Clare

Anasta
Divarenkan

MAGIC MONSTERS
Learn About Manners

by Jane Belk Moncure
illustrated by Linda Sommers

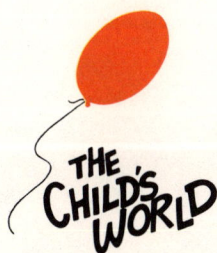

THE
CHILD'S
WORLD

ELGIN, ILLINOIS 60120

Distributed by Childrens Press, 1224 West Van Buren Street,
Chicago, Illinois 60607.

Library of Congress Cataloging in Publication Data

Moncure, Jane Belk.
  Magic monsters learn about manners.

  (Magic monster series)
  SUMMARY: Magic monsters demonstrate good
manners and how they apply to everyday situations.
    1. Etiquette for children and youth.
[1. Etiquette] I. Sommers, Linda. II. Title.
III. Series.
BJ1857.C5M6   395'.1'22   79-24528
ISBN 0-89565-118-1

MAGIC MONSTERS
Learn About Manners

When well-mannered monsters meet,
this is how they always greet.
They stand, shake hands. They smile and
   say,
"How are you today?"

To My Friend, Dino

Well-mannered monsters never think
of squeezing toothpaste in the sink.

6

They brush their teeth clean and bright
so they will sparkle in the night.

Before well-mannered monsters munch
on cactus bushes
for their lunch,

they wash their hands.

Then, they crunch
sweet cactus bushes
by the bunch.

9

No robot monster ever leaves a ring around
the tub.
With a monster brush, a rub, and a scrub,
he cleans the tub till it looks like new.
For, other Magic Monsters may want a clean
tub too.

Well-mannered ghosts never stuff clothes
behind the door.

Nor do witches throw pink polka-dot pajamas on the floor.

These monsters never jump on beds
with feathers flying round their heads.

And they don't have fluffy pillow
   fights,
except in the very middle of very stuffy
   nights!

ACHOO ! ! !

Well-mannered Monster Ellie knows
what to do with a drippy nose.
When she needs to sneeze or sniff,
she uses a tissue in a jiff.

When Magic Monsters take a trip,
they do not rush aboard the ship.
Each takes a turn. Each waits in line.
That works very, very fine!

Well-mannered monster girls and boys

share their magic monster toys.

Accidents happen. They always will.
Most things crack, or break, or spill.

Well-mannered monsters clean up messes
on table tops and floors and dresses.

When a well-mannered monster comes to
    tea,
he does not eat the company.
He does not bite or pinch or fight.
He is always quite polite.

He eats blackberry jam...
    on toast.

And when he leaves,
he thanks his host.

Little monsters can be seen
on city streets on Halloween.

Open the door and you will meet
well-mannered monsters who trick or treat.

Give them something good to eat
and they will vanish down the street.